A Match Made In Heaven

by

Theresa Wolmart

TRUE PERSPECTIVE
PUBLISHING HOUSE

A Match Made In Heaven

Copyright © 2012 by Theresa Wolmart

A Match Made in Heaven

Printed in the United States of America

ISBN 978-0-9846672-4-6

All rights are reserved solely by the author. The author declares that the contents are original and do not infringe on the rights of any other person.

No part of this book may be reproduced in any form except with permission from the author. The views in this book are not necessarily the views of the publisher.

Scripture quotations taken from the Amplified® Bible,
Copyright © 1954, 1958, 1962, 1964, 1965, 1987 by The Lockman Foundation
Used by permission." (www.Lockman.org)

Scriptures taken from the King James Version ®. Copyright © 1982 by Thomas Nelson, Inc. Used by
permission. All rights reserved.

Scripture quotations marked (NIV) are taken from the Holy Bible, New International Version®, NIV®. Copyright © 1973, 1978, 1984, 2011 by Biblica, Inc.™ Used by permission of Zondervan. All rights reserved worldwide.
www.zondervan.com.

DEDICATION

This book is dedicated to my sister-in-law, Joanne Nunziante, who was very instrumental in bringing me to the foot of the cross and to a knowledge of what the Blood of Jesus did for me.

Thanks Jo. I am forever indebted.

A Match Made In Heaven

SPECIAL THANKS

Thanks be to God, my Lord and Savior Jesus Christ, who gave me the zeal, strength and grace to carry out this assignment. God will never ask anything of us without giving us all we need, in order for us to obey and perform it to the fullest. He always causes us to triumph. Jesus, the lover of my soul, is my knight in shining armor.

Thanks so much to my husband Roy—"My Match Made In Heaven." Your support has been a great strength as I worked for hours, days and years on this project. Now, our story is out! I love you honey.

A very grateful thank you to my friend Graceann Rivera. We didn't know each other when we were in the same church years back. Facebook has changed that. You led me to your publisher, True Perspective. Thus, I found peace, and ended my search. God has brought us together. Let's keep this new friendship going. I'm loving it. God Bless You!

A very special thanks to Heather Dono. Words cannot express my gratitude for your expertise with your editing help. I remain more than impressed with your gift and talent—clearly given to you from above. Even more touching, was the wonderful time of fellowship we experienced. This is only the beginning. There will be more books. Love you dearly!

To my precious daughter Janine Leonhardt: From meeting Roy to marrying him, we exchanged roles. You were the acting parent, while I was the clueless child. We had ourselves some good laughs. I learned so much. The half of it has not even been told. The stories where I had you praying on your knees, we'll save for the movie. Thanks daughter. Love you too much!

To my friend Shelia McElroy, I still laugh from my belly when I recall the times we shared as I was believing God for Roy to ask me out. That kind of laughter does "good like a medicine." Our friendship has been just that—healing and medicine to my soul. Thank you for your devotion and your unconditional love. Thanks for believing in the Christ in me. Love you!

To my brother, Pastor Peter Nunziante: You were there for me anytime I called. "In a multitude of counselors, there is safety." You gave me your approval, guidance and good wishes—from the very beginning until the day you pronounced us as, "man and wife." Now, that's a privilege for any sister, especially an older sister! Love you!

A Match Made In Heaven

Thanks to everyone in this book who was mentioned by name, to those mentioned without being named—you know who you are—and to those not mentioned at all. There are many names and stories I could have included, but I had a goal to keep the book short. As I walk through this life, there are so many of you who are very dear to me.

From family to friends, to former bosses and co-workers, you are all very special to me.

Thanks for helping God make me who I am today. I treasure all of you.

A Match Made In Heaven

AUTOGRAPH PAGE

Autograph this book as a personal investment to yourself or the life of someone that God has put in your path on this life journey.

A Match Made In Heaven

TABLE OF CONTENTS

A Match Made In Heaven

PREFACE

This book is the story of a segment of my life. I felt mandated by God Almighty to write the true account of certain years of my life. Thus, I had to obey the inspiration that came upon me from *on High*.

I originally titled the book, "That Still Small Voice," but that "still small Voice" came to me one morning and inspired me to change the title to "A Match Made In Heaven." Throughout the pages of this book, I continually refer to "that still small Voice," and how He has directed my path. It was that same Voice that brought about the union between me and my husband, Roy. "That still small Voice" was responsible for the match made in heaven, which you will read about in the pages to follow.

This story begins when my ex-husband left after 27 years of marriage. That devastation caused me to recall the God who wooed me years before I even met my ex-husband and married him. Throughout high school and college, the Holy Spirit moved upon me until that glorious day where I became *born again*. Through my divorce, throughout all the hurt and the pain, I was reminded of the faithfulness of that great God, the One and Only God who brought me to a place of healing and health.

At this point, the story becomes light and funny, explaining the way I met my present husband until we married.

A Match Made In Heaven

The account you are about to read is one for the storybooks. Most love stories are fictional, where the reader enjoys a make-believe fairytale. However, my love story is true. In the pages of this book, you will meet the God who never fails; you will experience His love, His mercy and even His sense of humor. Although my story may seem *too good or too funny to be true*, everything I've written is the actual events of my life.

I purposely wrote this book short, sweet and easy to read. So join me on this little journey. I'm sure after you're finished, you will agree with me and say: *"To God be the Glory."*

CHAPTER ONE

GOD AND GOD ALONE

"...I will put My laws in their minds and write them on their hearts. I will be their God, and they will be My people. No longer will a man teach his neighbor, a man his brother, saying, 'Know the Lord,' because they will all know Me, from the least of them to the greatest."
Hebrews 8: 10 & 11 (NIV)

A Match Made In Heaven

God and God Alone

"*I*'ll always love you. I'll always have a place in my heart for you. You are the mother of my three children," my husband muttered as he exited the front door.

"Then, why are you leaving?" I asked. Puzzled, hurt and confused, I added, "Give me back my 30 years. Give them back right now!"

But still, he left. It was 1999, and I was 47.

What would I do? How would I pay the financial overhead? How would I be able to function alone?

I had known my husband since age 18, and really didn't know much else. I was young and by age 20 I was married with my first child. Although life with him was rather rough at times, as in any marriage, I believed in the marriage covenant we made before God. I was sure we would grow old together.

Despite the ups and downs, over time, I grew to unconditionally love him.

After 27 years of marriage, here I stood at the door asking him to reconsider. However, he insisted that he felt an overwhelming compulsion to leave. He, then, walked out of the house, out of the marriage and even walked away from his plumbing business.

A Match Made In Heaven

Thoughts flooded my mind. This was not what God had intended for us. What was he doing? What was he thinking? I walked inside my living room and sat down and began to reflect back to my high school days, even before I met my soon-to-be ex-husband.

I was a senior in high school preaching "Darwin's Theory of Evolution." I tried to persuade people that they evolved from an amoeba. I was raised a Catholic and knew *about* Jesus, but didn't *know* Jesus. Therefore, the reality of what His blood did for me was not a realization yet.

One day in high school, I ordered a Bible from the book club I had joined. When it arrived, I was excited to read it. I opened it to the first book of the Bible, Genesis 1:1, and read: "In the beginning God created the heaven and the earth." (*King James Version*)

I thought, wow, how profound and interesting. I was intrigued and thought, I *must* read this book. So, I left it out on my desk in my bedroom.

My dad came in to ask me something and saw the Bible. "That's not a Holy Catholic Bible," he said. "Where did you get this from?"

I was taken back a bit. My dad never went to church so what did it matter that I didn't buy a Holy Catholic Bible?

"From the book club," I answered. "It's a King James Bible. Why, are there different kinds of Bibles?"

"Yes," he replied, "Throw it away."

I guess he was afraid that I would get involved in some kind of cult or something. (Ironically, my father is a born-again believer today and thinks very differently.) However, I was an obedient girl and feared disobeying my dad. At first, I put it away in my closet. Then after a few days, I threw it away. Even though I did as I was told, I so wanted to read the Bible in its entirety. Yet all I had was that one verse: "In the beginning, God created the heaven and the earth."

I believe the Holy Spirit gave me the desire to buy the Book in order for me to learn that truth. The Bible tells us that the Word of God doesn't come back void but that it accomplishes what it sets out to do. It did indeed accomplish what it was set out to do; it broke the deception I was under concerning evolution.

A year later, I went on to college. One night as I was sitting on the floor in the middle of my bedroom studying, the Holy Spirit came over me with great conviction. I stood up, opened the window and noticed how beautiful the stars were.

I yelled out the window, "I believe you were born of the Virgin Mary and I believe Moses parted the Red Sea. I will never again preach the theory of evolution." The seed was sown. The revelation of Genesis 1:1 had taken root. No man had ever preached to me. Sometimes, it's God and God alone. Sometimes, God just does it all by Himself.

I am so thankful for the mercy, the goodness and the love of God in my life that I had come to know so early on. Even while helplessly watching my marriage crumble, I was alone but really not alone at all. I reflected on how my life with Jesus began. He called me until I finally answered. Since that moment, He never failed and never left me.

As I sat on the couch in the living room, I also recalled the marriage ceremony to my first husband. I remembered how I prayed, as my dad walked me down the aisle. I prayed and asked God to bless the union and the children we would have together. I recalled my thoughts to God: "I really don't know where to find You. I am here getting married in the church where I grew up, but I need to find You, God."

Suddenly, in that crowded church, the people on both sides became a blur as well as the priest at the altar. A cloudy-type mist that only my ex-husband and I saw appeared. God visited us that day and answered my prayer. Still, at this point in my life, no man ever preached to me. Yes, sometimes, it's God and God alone.

Remembering the start of our marriage and considering my impending divorce, I sat on the couch thinking, "This can't really be happening."

God and God Alone

God had so blessed us so many years before. Didn't my ex-husband remember that day or the countless blessings and interventions of God throughout the years?

Over the years, I've realized that the free will God gave us can get us into trouble. Sometimes, we make poor choices and decisions. The Scripture tells us, "There is a way that seems right unto a man, but the end of it is destruction." (*Proverbs 14:12 NIV*) We so need to learn the mind and heart of Christ and then follow it. His ways and thoughts are higher than ours.

Although my husband left, I still believed my marriage could be restored. I thought God would reunite us, even though my ex-husband married someone else for a season.

However, I came to know that God had other plans for me. We need the Holy Spirit to help us follow the Creator's blueprint and not our own.

I also found myself recalling my salvation experience back in 1976, when I asked Jesus to come and live in my heart. I acknowledged what He did for me at Calvary. I remembered that night so vividly. I was feeling such a *pull* from the Holy Spirit, I didn't know what to do about it. Some friends and family members were recently *"saved"* and constantly preaching to me. I thought they were all crazy and used to dread when they were at my door. Yet, I kept feeling that *tug* from the Holy Spirit.

A Match Made In Heaven

I called my soon to be sister-in-law Joanne and explained what I was experiencing. I asked her, "How can I be *saved?* What do I have to do?"

She replied, "You begin by thanking Jesus for dying on the cross for your sins."

It was as if a light bulb went off. "He died for me? Why didn't someone say that to me? All of you are saying this, that and the other thing. Everyone is shouting praises to God around my kitchen table, but no one told me that Jesus died for me!"

I quickly told Joanne that I had to hang up the phone. I sat in the middle of the kitchen floor and asked Jesus to come into my heart and I acknowledged that He died, rose again and that He sits at the right hand of the Father forever making intercession for me. I have never been the same since that night. The blood of Jesus became a reality to me. All the things I learned as a Catholic about Jesus made sense. Light was shed on my thinking. My spirit came alive. I had been *born again*. Yes, sometimes it's God and God alone, with, a little help from your soon to be sister-in-law.

The Gospel is simple. Sometimes it's so simple that we can miss it. Throughout my relationship with Christ, I have made it a practice to do what I learned that night in 1976 and what the Apostle Paul tells us: to preach Jesus crucified and risen again. My life was changed through the knowledge of the blood of Jesus that paid the price for my sins: past, present and future. When I went to church, I also learned that His stripes and beatings paid for my sickness and disease. What GOOD NEWS!!!

As I sat there in my living room, with my husband of 27 years closing the front door behind him, I felt devastated, forsaken and stabbed in the back. However, I found myself thanking Jesus for giving me the grace to consistently pursue Him all these years.

Psalm 56:3(*KJV*) came into my mind, "What time I am afraid, I will trust in Thee." I made the decision: I would trust Him. He had proved His faithfulness to me time and time again, and I knew He would continue to be faithful. I recalled the times that "still small Voice," that we read about in *1 Kings 19:12 KJV, "that gentle whisper"* directed me *(as the New International Version reads)*.

Several weeks before my ex-husband left, he was pressing me to quit my job. What if I would have listened to that voice? I would have been jobless and without a means of support as my marriage was ending. I am so thankful for that "still small Voice" that directs and enables us to discern correctly.

Please do not misunderstand me; I do not advocate a wife not listening to the plea of her husband because I believe she should. However, sometimes there is a higher authority that one must answer to. In this case, that "still small Voice" directed me to stay and not leave my job. God sees the end from the beginning and is able to spare us many hardships if we would only learn to hear and obey.

It is so important, so extremely vital for us to discern His voice and then to obey Him. I began learning this truth, in seed form, that night in college. Life changing experiences come from hearing and obeying God; in very simple matters and also the most complex of situations. His words are truly a "lamp unto our feet and a light unto our path." *Psalm 119:105(KJV.)* His wisdom is infinite and His "ways past finding out," as Paul tells us in *Romans 11:33* and I realized even more through a failing marriage.

CHAPTER TWO

SLEEPLESS NIGHTS TURN INTO A RICH PLACE

"We glory in tribulation also: knowing that tribulation worketh patience; And patience, experience: experience, hope: And hope maketh not ashamed; because the love of God is shed abroad in our hearts by the Holy Ghost which is given to us."
Romans 5:3 (KJV)

"I wait for the Lord, my soul waits, and in His word I put my hope. My soul waits for the Lord more than watchman wait for the morning."
Psalm 130: 5&6 (NIV)

"And the God of all grace, who called you to His eternal glory in Christ, after you have suffered a little while, will Himself restore you and make you strong, firm and steadfast. To Him be the power forever and ever. Amen" 1Peter 5:10-11 (NIV)

A Match Made In Heaven

Sleepless Nights Turn Into A Rich Place

J couldn't sleep for weeks. My mind wouldn't go to sleep. I never thought this would happen to me. I was desperate for one night of complete rest. I was desperate for a night of sleep, a night of relief. However, nothing, except for tears flowing as a river from deep, deep pain within. No, sleep was not happening.

"Okay, so I must go through this process and I will get to the other side." I would often recite such words to myself. I would continually remind myself that God had never failed me and that He would not fail me this time. I had to constantly encourage myself in the Lord as David did in *I Samuel 30:6.*

After much deliberation, I decided to see a sleep therapist. The lack of sleep was causing my immune system to break down. I developed a recurring case of bronchitis, a sickness I had never had a problem with until this point in my life.

When considering my high-paced job and the hours spent behind the wheel to get to and from work, I had no choice but to agree on taking sleeping pills for a season. However, even with all this help, I would awake in the middle of the night and not be able to fall back to sleep.

Determined not to allow this to devastate me, I would take out my Bible and declare: "I'll not put this Book down until you speak to me, Lord." I was desperate and I knew that His words would bring life, healing, wholeness and strength. I knew that one Word from His throne would make a world of difference. Sometimes I would fall asleep on my Bible and then awaken to His voice of encouragement. The scripture I'd wake up to, staring me right in the face would be the one that changed the atmosphere. The Holy Spirit would literally come upon my chest cavity and minister comfort. I would so know that Jesus was there.

The Lord would also reveal to me intimate details of the marriage, separation and divorce that took place and would unravel truths to me. God was indeed a "very present help in trouble" as His Word says.

God spoke to David and gave him explicit instructions. *I Chronicles 28:19 (NIV)* reads: "...I have in writing from the hand of the Lord upon me, and He gave me understanding in all the details of the plan." It isn't a strange thing for the Lord who made the heavens and the earth to speak and comfort His people. God spoke to Adam and Eve in the garden. God spoke to Abraham, Isaac and Jacob. God spoke to Moses and God will speak to you! He speaks out of the pages of the Bible. For the Bible is a living, breathing Word.

Then, faith comes from hearing from God as Paul teaches us in *Romans 10:17.* After a faith infusion, from that vantage point, we view the same situation in a different light; from a different perspective. For the same waters that drowned the whole world brought Noah and his family to the top of the mountain where they were above the flood, above the devastation, above the turmoil. The ark, where they were safely shut in by God Himself, was their protection and that ark was a type of Christ! Anyone in Christ goes safely through the floods and storms of life.

It isn't at all a strange thing for God to come and minister comfort, love, hope and strength. God is love. Jesus, who is 100 percent God and 100 percent man, is a person who has been touched with all the temptations common to man. Jesus came as a human and walked this earth for 33 years in order for Him to be that merciful high priest and know how we feel in any given situation. (*See Hebrews 2: 17&18*) God will never allow us to be in any trial that could overtake us. He only allows what we can handle. (*See I Corinthians 10:13*)

God gave me wisdom on how to operate and keep my house. I took in boarders for a season. God gave me favor with my bosses and I received many raises in a short period of time, which was not the norm. I did balance transfers on credit cards and refinanced my home. Before my ex-husband left, I very often had to pay the mortgage with a huge late fee. However, after my divorce, miraculously, my mortgage was never late.

God proved to me that He was better than any earthly husband could ever be. The Scripture, *Isaiah 54:5* became real to me: "For thy Maker is thy husband, the Lord of Host is His name and thy

29

Redeemer, the Holy One of Israel..." (*KJV*) All my bills were now paid on time or before time. I began to be established all on my own, without any natural help or aid. I was learning how to be independently dependent on God. What a glorious place I was coming into.

Success was happening and I started to see light at the end of the tunnel. However, some days I would wonder why the pain was still so prominent. At times, I would feel victorious and other days the ache was so severe that it felt as if I were missing limbs.

Mark 10:19 (*NIV*) speaks of marriage as the following: "therefore what God has joined together, let man not separate." When God joins a man and a woman they become one, so when man tries to pull that union apart, especially after 27 years of marriage, it literally feels as if a leg or an arm is being pulled out of joint. How true.

God is a covenant God. Marriage is a sacred and holy covenant where vows are repeated in the sight of God and man. What happened to that understanding? How sad, that so many do not understand the importance of keeping vows.

Yes, the pain was still so alive and the crying would happen at any time or anywhere but, as always, the Holy Spirit would immediately be on the scene, ministering to me and surrounding me with His love. When reading *Jeremiah 29:11*, Jesus would always reassure me how much He truly loved me and of the plans He had for me--plans to keep me and to give me a good future. He would speak to me, out of the Word, and show me that He had plans to prosper me in body, soul and spirit.

The sleepless nights were getting better, but still occurred from time to time. One night, in particular, became a turning point. As I awoke in the middle of the night, God ministered to me out of *Psalm 115:14 and 15* and showed me that He would increase both me and my children, more and more. I took that promise and happening to heart and stood on it. I don't know what I would have done had it not been for the Bible that brought life to me on a daily basis; the same Bible my dad had me throw away so many years earlier.

During the half hour drive to and from work, my car became my altar. I kept my focus on Jesus. I didn't look to the right or to the left. I went to work and church, out to eat with my God-given girlfriends, or, I would wrap myself in my grandbabies. I had a shield up saying, "No one allowed flirting here. No one allowed in."

I thought I would remain alone, rather single. I could not imagine life with another man, and that was okay. I had peace, success, security and a sense of self-worth. Jesus brought me to a place where I now was a whole, healed individual "leaning upon her beloved."

A Match Made In Heaven

I want you to know that this secret, special, privileged place is available. You need to be a whole person before you allow a man or a woman into your life. The man or woman must be a whole person as well. Being equally yoked means two whole people who are walking with God.

Paul tells us in *II Corinthians 6:14 (KJV)* "Be ye not unequally yoked together with unbelievers..." Marriage and life has hardships. With the right partner and the third person, Jesus, (making the three-fold cord, which is not easily broken - *Ecclesiastes 4:12 (KJV)*), there isn't anything that cannot be conquered.

God promised to give Abraham and Sarah a son; even with Sarah being well beyond child-bearing years. They waited and believed for God's promise. But after some time had passed, Sarah weakened, causing Abraham to concede to her wishes of going in to her handmaiden to bear a son for them. Thus, Ishmael was born. If you read the account in Genesis, you will see that this decision caused much grief and pain.

Yes, God blessed Ishmael, because that's just the way God is. However, the promise, which was Isaac, was the real blessing and intent of God from when the Word was first spoken.

Eventually, when the appointed time had come, Sarah did indeed conceive and Isaac was born. Too many times people settle for Ishmael instead of waiting for Isaac and they put extra burden upon their shoulders.

Sleepless Nights Turn Into A Rich Place

Do you know when you are ready for God to bring that special person into your life He is preparing for you? You are ready when you do not care if Jesus ever brings anyone in your life, because you'll believe God is enough. When you have that testimony, *watch out now,* God is about to move on your behalf.

A Match Made In Heaven

CHAPTER THREE

OKAY GOD, I'M READY NOW

"The law of the Lord is perfect reviving the soul. The statues of the Lord are trustworthy, making wise the simple. The precepts of the Lord are right, giving joy to the heart. The commands of the Lord are radiant, giving light to the eyes."

Psalm 19:7-8 (NIV)

"I will instruct thee and teach thee in the way which thou shalt go: I will guide thee with Mine eye."

Psalm 32:8 (KJV)

35

A Match Made In Heaven

Okay God, I'm Ready Now

*S*ix years passed. It was now February 2005. I was packing to go on a church cruise, a cruise that my dear friend had encouraged me to book. She insisted that I needed to do this for myself, no matter what the financial cost. So, after much persuasion, I agreed and we booked a balcony room together. A few weeks before the cruise, she suddenly passed on to be with the Lord. Other friends and family members were trying to talk me out of going. They insisted that I would be grieving for her resulting in a terrible time on the cruise.

Even through my grief, I knew my friend would want me to go. She was the one who convinced me to treat myself with this vacation. Then came "that still small Voice"; and that Voice told me to go ahead with my plans. Of course, that was the Voice that I obeyed.

It's not the voice from your head. It's not the voice from your loved ones (although many times that voice does work through others). It's not the voice from your closest friends. It is rather, that "still small Voice" from within that brings direction, as a rudder on a ship directs the vessel. Yes, it is that prompting, that "gentle whisper," that you can only hear with your spiritual ears, which confirms the way every time you listen for it. So, I packed cheerfully, knowing that this was the right move to make. While I was packing, I prayed a prayer that I didn't expect to pray. I prayed: "Lord, I'm ready now. Send me someone. Since I only go to work and church, why not send me an usher?"

I went on the cruise and had a blast. I made new friends with people from the church, whom I had never had a chance to really get to know. It was my first time out of the country and I really was appreciating the witnessing of my new healed self, my whole self, my independent self. It was glorious!

I stayed in a room by myself and enjoyed the luxury of a king size bed and treasured the alone time–it was just me and Jesus. It was truly a time of refreshing and indeed a time of transition. For that, I am sincerely thankful to my dear friend.

On the night before the cruise ended, our church group had a farewell meeting. A prophet was on the cruise with us. He shared and spoke about some things the Lord had placed on his heart. He said, God spoke to him that there were many single women whom God was going to bring companionship to. He also shared, that this time next year, there would be marriages in the church that I was attending.

I knew this word was for me, so I slapped my new-found friend, who was standing next to me, on the arm and declared: "I'm getting married next year at this time!" The prophet continued on and shared: "Because God was put first, God saw the heart and God was going to bring reward."

Okay God, I'm Ready Now

I received the prophetic word by faith. I wasn't even sure that I wanted to get married and I didn't remember praying, "Lord, send me someone" right before I left for the cruise. **But God remembered**, and I believe it was God who prompted me to pray the prayer in the first place.

For we know not what to pray, but the Spirit prays through us. He moves us to pray for His will to be done in our lives. When those of us who belong to Him, pray and believe Him, according to His will and according to His Word, there isn't anything that He will withhold from us. It is His desire to give us the kingdom. He said, "If you remain in Me and My words remain in you, ask whatever you wish, and it will be given you." (*John 15:7 NIV*)

When I returned home from the trip, I went to church. In the section where my family always sat, a new usher had been assigned. He greeted me and led me to my seat.

As the weeks went on, Roy, the new usher, was there serving in the house of God. My family and I began to get to know him and to talk with him. He sat right next to me. One day, my daughter Janine was sitting behind me and she questioned me, "Who is that man? I see something here."

I responded, "What? Are you kidding me? A good-looking man like that has to be married."

She replied, "I see something over the both of

39

you. I think it's a marriage mantle."

I knew that Janine wasn't one to say anything as such if it were not the real thing. However, I thought, "Lord, is she seeing correctly?" She inquired of her husband Lance about Roy. Lance knew Roy and confirmed that he was not married. Janine then relayed the information to me, but I still was not sure that there was any truth to any of this.

Not long after, the flirting started. I thought he was flirting, but then again, I really didn't know what flirting was. I was confused and scared, but I began to flirt back. At least I thought I was flirting back. I really wasn't sure how all that stuff worked.

When the flirting increased, and it became visible to those around us, *I inquired of the Lord.* I went into my bedroom, sat in the middle of my bed Indian style, and I lifted it up to the Lord saying, "Lord Jesus, there is a flirting going on here. What is up with this? What is happening with this man Roy?"

Well, all of a sudden, stronger than ever before, the Holy Spirit moved on me and engulfed me in such a way that I felt as if I were elevated off my bed. There was a witness of witnesses letting me know that God's hand and approval was on this relationship. I was awestruck! I actually knew from that encounter with God, that we would be married. In the twinkling of an eye, God can change a situation. When you least expect it, *suddenly*, things turn around and life takes a shift.

I called Janine to tell her about this happening in the spirit. I expressed to her that she was indeed correct in that marriage mantle that she saw. Then she mentioned to me something that I had totally forgotten about. She said, "Don't you remember you prayed and expressed to God that you were ready, and asked Him to send you someone, and why not an usher?"

Wow! I didn't remember that at all! I didn't even put it together after I came home from the cruise, I said the prophecy was for me and that I was getting married, but I felt as if I was half joking. *God was not joking, but rather very serious.* We better watch out what we pray for: we just might get it. Jesus has such a cool sense of humor.

Okay, so now I know that I am going to marry this usher named Roy. I didn't even know his last name yet. So, what do I do now? I certainly can't let him in on this secret. So, I guess I'll just keep flirting and take it from there.

So, flirt is what we did for months – flirt, flirt, flirt. At the end of the Mother's Day service at church, the mothers are invited up to take a flower. I didn't go up. Roy came to me at my seat with a cute little bouquet of red flowers. He also always helped with the grandbabies Sunday mornings when they were in attendance. He was gracious, kind, polite and complimentary. However, my

A Match Made In Heaven

constant thought was "When oh when will he ask me out on a date?" I was getting anxious and concerned. March, April, May, June and still just flirting. What was up with this guy?

Then one day at work, while sitting at my desk, the Holy Spirit moved on me and prompted me to go to the concert at Jones beach where the church band was ministering. Originally, I had planned on going with my lady friends but they canceled out due to an extreme heat wave with severely high temperature. I didn't want to drive there alone, yet I knew the impression I was getting from God.

Then my daughter Janine called and asked me if I would drive her there. She explained, her husband was working and she was just too far along in her pregnancy and too swollen to drive. Well, okay then. I saw how God was setting this whole thing up. However, what was He setting up? I hadn't a clue!

As soon as we arrived, I knew the reason I had to be there. Roy greeted us at the entrance. He was greeting and seating all those who attended the concert. Wow! I was thanking Jesus for prompting me to go to that event. Roy immediately got a chair for Janine to sit in, seeing her very pregnant state.

When we left to go home, he said to me, "Talk to you the next time I see you." I figured that to be the next church service but he wasn't there. Nor was he at the next one. Oh my, what happened to him? Where was he? Weeks passed and still no Roy.

A Match Made In Heaven

CHAPTER FOUR

THE PHONE CALL

"The Lord will fulfill His purpose for me..."

Psalm 138:8 (NIV)

A Match Made In Heaven

The Phone Call

I just didn't get it. Where was he? Why didn't he say something that night at Jones Beach? Many people in the section where we sat in church were inquiring about his absence. He was so well liked and he was very missed. People were very concerned. I was concerned, to say the least. Was it his family? Had his mom or dad taken ill? My goodness. Did he fall off the face of the earth?

Finally, after the fourth week of no show, my son-in-law Lance offered to call him and ask if everything was okay. I agreed that it was a good idea. After all, it wasn't me that would be making the call. So, Lance called him, but it didn't go down as I thought it would. He called and got his voicemail, so he left a message.

The message went something like this: "Hi Roy, this is Lance calling. My mother-in-law has been concerned that you haven't been in church and she wanted me to check on you and see if all is well. She is very old-fashioned and would not make the call herself. You may call me back to let me know. Better yet, if you would like, why not call her?" He then left my cell phone number.

When he called to tell me what happened, I was so embarrassed. I exclaimed, "What did you do that for? Are you crazy? Now, what do I do? What if he really calls me?" My son in-law chuckled.

A Match Made In Heaven

This all occurred on a Sunday afternoon. I kept my cell phone handy, in case he called. However, no phone call came. By Monday, I went to work and was so busy I totally forgot about the phone call. Then my son Adam called to talk to me about a basement renovation, which was going on in my home. He told me that the contractor couldn't finish but another contractor would be calling me momentarily to discuss the completion of the job.

After hanging up with my son, my cell phone rang. I looked and didn't recognize the number. I figured it was the new contractor so I answered, expecting just that. "Hello," I said. I then heard, "Theresa?"

"Yes, this is Theresa," I replied. I was sure that this person would than proceed to tell me that he was the contractor Adam recommended.

However, I heard this instead, "This is Roy."

Oh my! It was him! Oh my goodness, what do I say? My mind was flooded. I was shaking, panicking and lost for words. "Oh, hi," I replied. "How are you? Where have you been? Did you fall off the face of the earth? Many of us have been worried."

He laughed and responded, "I'm down South visiting my son and his family in Texas. He is about to leave for Iraq, so we are spending time together."

"Oh," I said, "that's great." Now, this Italian girl was hardly ever at a loss for words, but this time I was tongue-tied. I didn't know what to say next. This is what came out: "Thanks so much for the phone call. It was very nice of you to call and let me know what was going on."

He responded, "Thanks so much for caring. I'll see you in about a week."

After we hung up, I began verbally beating myself up. There it was. A **real phone call!** He called **me** back, not Lance. But here I was tongue-tied and frozen, cutting off the phone call before it got rolling. What was wrong with me? I was very upset. I then began to rehearse in my mind what I would ask him the next time I saw him. Did he have any more children? How many grandchildren did he have? I was coming up with my own mental list. I wasn't going to let what happened with this first phone call, occur again. No, I had to find a way to become bold and just be me. I saved his cell phone number in my phone but, of course, I wouldn't dare dial the number.

When he returned to church and greeted me I was indeed bolder and I did ask those questions. The flirting then continued and even went up a notch or two. One day he threw me a kiss goodbye from across the aisle. I blew one back to him. Wow, I couldn't believe I actually did that! Look at this bold, outgoing me! Woo hoo! I was having fun and it felt so good to be carefree.

Suddenly, he came racing up the aisle after me. He hugged me and kissed me on my cheek and said, "I don't like long-distance kisses!" I was shocked, stunned and so excited. I left laughing and just about floating on air. I was elated, but couldn't help thinking, "When will he ask me out? How long will this continue before a date happens?"

From the very beginning of this whole *Roy* matter, I had been counseling with my brother Peter, (a pastor for many years). I told him everything and kept giving him updates. He agreed to pray for me about this issue. He liked Roy and gave me his blessing. He also told me to "have fun."

I kept complaining to Peter about the fact that Roy hadn't asked me out. My brother knew how old-fashioned I was. Although he understood and agreed, he expressed to me that in this day sometimes women ask men out.

"What? Not me!!!!" I declared.

He laughed and said, "I'm not saying that you should ask him out, I'm just giving you an option because this is a new day and people do things differently."

Not me. I would not do that. I was going to wait and see. He had to ask me out soon. I mean, how much longer will the flirting go on? It was at this point, six months.

CHAPTER FIVE

THE DREAM

"...so He shall open, and none shall shut: and He shall shut, and none shall open. And I will fasten him as a nail in a sure place..."

Isaiah 22: 22&23 (KJV)

A Match Made In Heaven

The Dream

*I*t was the first week in September 2005 and I had two beautiful grandchildren. Both my daughters were scheduled to have C-sections, so I took two weeks off from work and took care of my two daughters and their new babies.

Now that Roy was back, I wanted so badly to go to church, but I had to take care of my family. Between visiting them at hospitals and then their homes, I was exhausted. I really didn't have much time to think of anything other than diapers, bottles, stitches and caring for the other three grandchildren. When I arrived home each night, I was soon knocked out into a very deep sleep.

One night, I had a dream I knew was from God. Most of the time you can discern the difference between a dream from God and one that is insignificant. Dreams from God are very distinct and leave an everlasting impression.

This dream was set in a home where I lived in Brooklyn, N.Y., when I was a young girl. It was an upstairs apartment and at the top of the stairs my mom had a table and a picture centered on the wall over the table. She always kept things neat, clean and pretty. The picture was crooked, so I took it off the wall to fix it and hang it straight.

My ex-husband was there with me and he tried to help me but could not hang it straight. While we were attempting to fix it, my dad walked out the door, down the steps and out the front doorway. Then, I turned the picture over and showed my ex-husband that there were two places for two nails. At that point, I realized the reason the picture failed to hang straight. There was only one nail holding it up. I said, "One won't work," and went into the living room which was right off that landing.

As my dream continued, my cell phone rang and to my surprise, it was Roy. I was so excited. I ran into the bathroom to talk to him. My ex-husband kept asking me, "Who is that?" "Who is that?"

"Ssssshhhhhh," I responded as I opened the bathroom door and then quickly shut it again. Then I awoke. Wow! I knew that was definitely God showing me something. How interesting. What a faithful God!

Later on, at my daughter Lauren's house, I was doing my grandma thing and my friend Ro called to congratulate me on the birth of the two babies. As we spoke, I shared the dream with her. I just couldn't shake it off. Immediately, she said she felt a witness in her spirit and that God showed her exactly what it meant. She said, "What was crooked would now be made straight. Roy is the other nail needed to make the picture hang properly." Wow, I liked that interpretation!

That evening, as I was reading in my devotional time with the Lord, the Scriptures in

The Dream

Isaiah 22:22-23 KJV shot out at me and I was stunned. I read, "And the key of the house of David will I lay upon his shoulder; so he shall open, and none shall shut; and he shall shut, and none shall open. And I will fasten him as a **nail** in a sure place." There it was: the other **nail**! I knew that I knew that I knew that God was assuring me that Roy was to be my husband, that He was going to put him over my family and that He was going to bless him. There it was again, that Voice, that direction, that anointing that teaches us all things. What a mighty and a faithful loving God!

At this point, I remembered that a few weeks prior Roy had received a word from another visiting prophet that was ministering in a church service. He pulled out Roy and told him to stand. He then told him that he was about to receive a great harvest and that God was going to bless him. When Roy received that word, I knew by the spirit that the harvest was, in part, my family. I remember chuckling inside. I even remember telling my lady friends that I think the blessing the prophet meant was that Roy was going to inherit a whole family--mine!

Now, as I type these events something else comes to mind. After we were married awhile, the head pastor at church pulled Roy out one night at a prayer meeting and told Roy God was going to open doors for him. He told him not to look to the past where doors were shut in his face, but to know that God was going to do this for him. As I was typing the details of the dream and the Scriptures concerning the dream, I realized that back then God was showing me that He was going to open doors for Roy that I didn't see until today. Just as His Scripture says, "...so He shall open, and none shall shut..."

CHAPTER SIX

THE TEXT MESSAGE

"...for He gives [blessings] to His beloved in sleep."

Psalm 127:2 (The Amplified Bible)

"My Sheep hear My voice, and I know them, and they follow Me."

John 10:27 (KJV)

A Match Made In Heaven

The Text Message

Two weeks passed and I'm finished with all my grandma duties. It is a Friday night and I get all decked out to go to church. I was going to see Roy! My friend Shelia was at my house eating dinner with me, and as soon as we were done, we were going to church.

We each took our own car. That way, after church, we could just go home separately. We lived in two different directions. I arrived in the church parking lot before she did, so I sat in my car and waited for her to arrive. After she pulled in the spot next to me, she stayed in the car to fix her makeup. When I saw her opening her car door, I proceeded to get out of mine.

While the two of us started walking from our cars to the front of the church building, Roy pulled into the parking lot. When you consider that this church has a congregation in the thousands with several parking lots, the chances of Roy parking right next to us is small.

Shelia and I paused and waited for him to catch up to us. (We had to be polite you know!) Roy greeted me with a kiss and said, "You really look good in pink." Oh my! He smelled so good! I liked his cologne. He inquired about the newest grandbabies. He said he figured that was why I hadn't been in church. I showed him pictures that I had ready in my purse. He showed us pictures of a great niece that was just born in his family. We had a great conversation and then the three of us walked into church together.

After the church service was ended, we spoke some more in the back of the church. Roy asked me if I would be there on Sunday and I responded, "Of course." My friend Shelia was sensing that he wanted to ask me if I would like to go for coffee or something. That didn't happen. We then said goodnight and Shelia and I walked out to our cars together.

"Girl," she said, "You should just ask him to come back to your house for tea or something." She was willing to come back to the house with me, had I invited him, but I would NOT do that!

"He has to ask me out," I declared.

"Okay then, have it your way," she replied.

A few days after that night, I had another dream. In the dream, Roy sent me a text message. I shared the dream with my daughter Janine. She thought it was imperative that she teach me how to text. I laughed and informed her that, "People our age don't text."

She replied, "You know you get dreams from God. You need for me to teach you how to do this."

I laughed and laughed. I thought the dream was just a silly one. I did not think this, too, was God leading me. Sure enough, a few days later, after I awoke and went into the kitchen to check my phone for messages, I saw something strange on the phone. It appeared as if it were some sort of message but certainly not a voicemail. I pressed "OK."

Lo and behold, a text message popped up. Whoop, whoop! It was from (guess who?) Roy!! It read: "HAVE A BLESSED DAY!"

I started to jump around my kitchen saying, "Lord, the dream **WAS** from You! Janine was correct, but I didn't allow her to teach me. Now, I don't know how to respond!" I tried to text back, but I couldn't figure it out. So I called Janine and left a voicemail stating what just took place. I apologized for calling at six in the morning. However, I knew she would understand my urgent message and come to my aid. She called me back as soon as she heard the voicemail and walked me through a quick lesson.

I texted back, "And you, too." I went to work smiling from ear to ear. Wow, a text message! I thought for sure we were close to that date that I was waiting for. I mean, I figured that after this he would definitely ask me out. But I was wrong.

A few days later, while at my desk at work, I felt the inspiration of the Holy Spirit come to me once again concerning the *Roy* issue. Yes, there it was again--that "still small Voice," that prompting within, that voice that His sheep hear, that voice that is so distinct you just know it is Him and not you.

A Match Made In Heaven

It came to me with a great *knowing* and I heard in my know-er, my spirit, "Invite Roy to a family dinner." I was stunned and very taken back. I replied, "Lord, I don't want to do that, I want him to ask me out on a date. Lord, come on. This isn't fair. I'm too embarrassed to do that." Since it came with such great inspiration and since I knew that I knew, beyond a shadow of a doubt that it was His voice, I really had no choice but to obey God.

The Scripture tells us in *I Samuel 15:22 (KJV)* "...to obey is better than sacrifice..." Sometimes God will ask things of us that are contrary to our thinking and our personalities. I knew from experience that obeying the Lord is always the way to go, for He had my best interest in mind. His wisdom always surpasses mine. I didn't quite understand why God would allow me to humiliate myself but this ole'-school woman was going to have a major breakthrough with her shyness and beliefs. I was just going to simply obey God.

It was very close to my daughter Lauren's birthday (September 28th). The Sunday before her birthday, I decided to make a family dinner and cook my famous Italian meatballs. When I got up enough nerve, I called Roy in order to invite him to the gathering. He didn't pick up, so I left him a voicemail. A few days passed, and I didn't hear back from him. I knew that cell phones can be tricky.

I often get voicemails days after they were sent, so I decided to try one more time. I announced

The Text Message

to the Lord, "Here I go Lord. I'm obeying You-- inviting the man to dinner and leaving a second message. The menu is planned and the family is coming, but he has not responded yet." Thus, I left a second message.

I was at my daughter Janine's house helping her bathe her baby Alexa for the first time. The baby's belly button had fallen off. I had just finished dressing my beautiful new granddaughter when I heard my cell phone ring. I looked at the caller ID and to my pleasant surprise, it was Roy.

He explained that he got my message and that he would be happy to join us for dinner. We had a nice conversation. So it was set. After church on Sunday, Roy was having dinner with me and my family. By the way, he never did get the first voicemail. I'm so glad I tried again. Had I not persevered and obeyed that "still small Voice," I might still be waiting for a date.

Dinner went great. The babies were 2 and 3 weeks old. I made all my best dishes and set the best table ever. I made a birthday cake for Lauren and we had a great family day with Roy. I was nervous, so I just went about my busy way. He kept coming over to me requesting that I "Stop cleaning up."

He asked me to "Come sit down." He also continually offered to help me and insisted on throwing out the trash. He complimented the cooking, the family, the house, etc. Realizing I was allowing my nervousness to cause me to be rude, I stopped all my chores. I then joined Roy and went out on the back deck with him.

We sat and talked for a long time. I asked him many questions. He explained a lot about his life. I, too, answered many of his questions concerning my life. During the months in church, we did exchange much information about each other but this day we really brought it up another notch or two. This day, something special was happening. I remember looking at him in admiration and watching his every movement.

I remember thinking that I could very easily love this man. Before he left that night, he gave me a hug and thanked me again for dinner. I then walked him out to his car. I was on cloud nine. I had that "still small Voice" of direction to thank for this happening. I was grateful that God prodded me to put down my backward flesh and ask the man to dinner. At this point, I surely thought he would ask me out on a date.

My daughter Janine then informed me what was to happen next was a phone call. I said to her, "You mean there are rules to this stuff?" I was so not knowing any of this. She explained that if he truly enjoyed himself and wanted to continue on into a relationship, he would call and thank me for dinner.

I thought that was strange, since he already thanked me but I felt she knew better. I then waited for his phone call. Monday and Tuesday came and went and still no phone call. However, on Wednesday, there it was--a phone call. I was finishing up at work and getting ready to call it a day when my cell phone rang. I recognized the number and happily answered. Yep, you guessed it, Roy thanked me for dinner.

I wondered how in the world Janine knew all this and the way it all worked. There really were rules and I was hoping that the next rule was a date. Instead of a date, Roy asked me if I would be in church that night; he knew that (at that time) I was playing piano for a small Wednesday night gathering. I told him I would be there. He said that he was thinking of going and that he may see me there. That was one service that Roy didn't attend so I was super excited at the fact that now he wanted to go. I was thinking maybe he would show up and ask me on a DATE!

Usually, on Wednesdays I would go home after work, eat dinner and then freshen up before going to church. This Wednesday was different, because Roy would perhaps show up. So, I went home, ate quickly and then showered and changed into fresh makeup and clothes. I made sure I looked my best and was ready to meet him.

But he never showed. I reasoned to myself that I did indeed get that phone call, which according to Janine showed interest. At this point, I was ecstatic that we even got this far. Certainly a date had to be close.

A Match Made In Heaven

My friend Shelia called to find out how the Sunday dinner went. I filled her in on all the newest details. She asked me, "What's the man's last name?"

"I don't know," I replied.

"Girl, what do you mean you don't know the man's last name? This man is going to be your husband and you don't know his last name?" We laughed and laughed. I didn't have a clue what my last name was going to be. I was still waiting to go on a date.

That Friday night, I went to church, but I didn't see Roy there. I decided to use this new method of communicating that Janine taught me. I texted Roy. I got really bold and I typed: "Missed you in church tonight. When are we going to go out somewhere?"

He texted back: "I was there. See you on Sunday."

Now, I was ticked. I did the dinner thing. He did the phone call follow-up. What was the problem? I couldn't believe that I actually asked him such a bold question and then? The nerve! He didn't have the decency to answer me. I was so upset. I didn't hear from him over the weekend.

Then in church on Sunday, he was flirting more than ever. After service was over, he put his arm out for me to put my arm in and we walked up the aisle together. My daughter Janine bumped into us as we approached the lobby and asked us what we were doing. I explained to her that I had nothing to do and was probably just going home. I thought for sure that Roy would then invite me to lunch, but instead he asked, "Are you coming back to church tonight?"

Now, I was fuming! He didn't answer my text, the door is opened for him to ask me to lunch and he wants to know if I'm coming back to church! I looked at him and said with an attitude, "No, I'm NOT coming back tonight!" I then walked out the door and to my car.

I called Shelia and asked her if she wanted to go to lunch. We went to Ruby Tuesdays and I kept yacking and complaining and moaning and groaning. She tried to make me understand that text messages and emails are not to be trusted. She thought that perhaps he didn't receive the whole message. Her suggestion was that I should go back to church that night and confront him.

I was not doing anything of the sort. We went back to my house after lunch and I continued my rampage. I was ticked. And that was putting it lightly! Shelia refused to stay and listen to my nonsense about the man who was to be my husband, the man whose last name I didn't even know.

Shelia has a way of making me laugh at all times, but she really did leave. That's Shelia, and I thank God for friends like her. At that point, I decided to put on some scrubs and clean my house.

A Match Made In Heaven

I figured I would just clean one room after another. I had such energy over this man Roy whatever his last name was. I had to work it out. Thus, I was determined to clean my way out of it.

I cleaned a few rooms. Then my son and his girlfriend came in to visit with me. I figured it was a good time to take a break. My cell phone rang and it was Roy. I informed my son Adam and his girlfriend not to disturb me. I told them I was going in another room to take the call.

"Hello" I answered.

"Theresa," he began.

"Yes," I responded.

He proceeded to share that he was driving back to church and he couldn't get me off his mind. He said he had the feeling that I was upset. He said he was thinking about asking me to lunch, but he didn't want to interfere with my family functions.

I let him know that he should have asked me to lunch and that I was indeed upset that he didn't. I reiterated how I said to Janine that I had nothing to do and that I would probably just go home. He acknowledged that I did say that but he thought I really wanted to be with my family. I informed him that he was wrong and then I confronted him on the text message that he didn't answer.

"What text message?" he asked.

He explained that he only got the message that said, "I missed you in church."

The Text Message

It turns out the only time he ever texted before was the text he sent me, which was: "Have a Blessed Day!" He thought that you can only text or receive one line messages. He was not aware that you could open up a text.

Shelia was right. She told me not to trust such communication. We had a good laugh. He then said the words I was impatiently awaiting: "We are going to go out all the time to a lot of places."

Roy apologized and asked me if we could just forget that weekend and continue from there. ("Well yeah," I thought. I mean the man was going to be my husband.)

I responded, "Okay, cool. I am so glad you called." After we hung up, I thought, "Hmm, I wonder what his last name is?"

Sure enough, when I called Shelia to tell her he called, that all was okay and that she was correct about emails and text messages, she asked me, "So what's the man's last name?"

"I don't know girl, give me a chance," I responded.

"Ask the man his name already!" she commanded.

We had a good laugh.

A Match Made In Heaven

CHAPTER SEVEN

THE PROPHET SAYS MARRIAGE MANTLE

"I am alert and active, watching over My Word to perform it."

Jeremiah 1:12 (The Amplified Bible)

A Match Made In Heaven

The Prophet Says Marriage Mantle

*A*fter all that drama, we all had a good laugh or two or three. Now, finally things were very different. Roy called me the very next day and came by after Bible School. He called me every day after that. Now that we're married, he still calls me all the time.

We began going out to dinner and movies. We talked and talked and talked. After a week or so passed, he picked me up for church instead of us meeting there. We became a couple and did everything together.

A few weeks passed and Shelia would not leave me alone about his last name, so, I texted him and asked him, "By the way, what is your last name?"

He responded, "Wolmart."

"Wow," I thought. Wolmart, that's interesting. I never expected to be a Wolmart. Roy apologized that his name had an 'O' in it instead of an 'A' in there. I laughed.

As soon as I could, (you guessed it), I called Shelia. I didn't want to hear her ask about Roy's last name any longer. She was excited when I told her, and exclaimed, "Wow, so your last name will be Wolmart!"

Shh," I said "Not too loudly girl! He doesn't know that yet."

A Match Made In Heaven

So, now our lives were getting intertwined. We were together all the time, until it was time for Roy to go home and go to sleep. If we weren't going out, I was cooking dinner.

Then came the day he took me home to meet his family. I was greatly received by his mom and dad and by his many siblings. (His dad has since gone home to be with the Lord. I am so glad I had a chance to meet him.)

Soon after, the same prophet that gave Roy the word about the great harvest he was about to receive came back to church. Roy was still ushering at the time, and he was told to stand up front and wait on the prophet. While the man of God was preaching his message, he stopped and turned to Roy and asked him if his wife was there and if so, to bring her up.

Roy replied, "I'm not married." We weren't dating all that long, so Roy just left it at that. He never mentioned that he was in fact in a *new* relationship. (After all, Roy had an inkling that we would be married, but he was not as positive as I was!) Then the prophet said to him, "You will be married. I see a marriage mantle over you."

I was sitting in my seat chuckling and so were my girlfriends. Shelia was whispering, "Here's his wife. She's over here," while pointing at me.

The prophet then announced to the whole congregation, "Women, he's available. Go to Roy.com."

The Prophet Says Marriage Mantle

Hmm, I thought, "No you don't!" All my friends were hysterical and the congregation went wild with laughter. This was the second witness for me concerning a marriage mantle. My daughter Janine saw it over us at the onset of our meeting; now it was the prophet sent from God!

How blessed I was that God would allow time, in the middle of a meeting, to confirm again this relationship was to be. I was sitting there thinking about the scripture, "...What is man that thou art mindful of him? Or the son of man that thou visitest him?" (*Hebrews 2:6 KJV*) It tells us in *I John 3 (KJV)*, "Behold what manner of love the Father hath bestowed upon us, that we should be called the sons of God..." I was overwhelmed with the love of God towards me and Roy.

God cares about the little things as well as the huge things. Everything about us concerns God. He takes joy being a part of every single facet of our lives. Jesus also likes having fun. I'm sure He had himself a few good laughs during the course of this whole happening. I was truly humbled at this point. That's what God's grace and love does, it humbles.

The Scripture tells us in *Romans 2:4 that* it is the goodness of God that leads us to repentance and in my experiences it is that goodness that brings humility. "Oh how He loves you and me!" There really isn't anything He won't do for those that are His as long as it is according to His Word. He'll move heaven and earth if He has to. He will move on your behalf when something is ordained and in His will. In *Jeremiah 1:12* we read that God is watching over His word to perform it! The *KJV* says*: "...* for I will hasten My word..." *The Amplified Bible* reads: "...for I am alert and active, watching over My word to perform it."

When we left church, Roy was in a bit of shock. We started discussing what happened and he was acting very scared and feeling the weight of the marriage mantle that was just pronounced over him. Roy admitted that he was very uncomfortable and that he really didn't know what to make of it. We spoke for a short time and then we went home.

After arriving at our homes we spoke on the phone. He was still expressing his uneasiness. I totally understood how he could be feeling; yet I wondered if I should then express some truths that I knew. Being the talkative Italian person that I am, I did just that.

I felt safer now that we were on the telephone. I began to share with him everything from the very beginning. I expressed to him the way God spoke to me and about the dreams I had and how God answered my "send me an usher prayer." I even told him about the marriage mantle my daughter discerned from the very start.

After he listened to me expound, he said he needed time to digest it all and needed to hang up. I was scared, but I knew deep down God was doing all this and that it was all going to be okay.

It was a long night for me. I was anxious to read my morning text from Roy. We always texted each other in the morning. He would write me beautiful encouraging words. (We still text all the time. It was a huge part of our coming together. Every time we text words of endearment it brings a rekindling.)

I waited patiently for the morning light. I didn't sleep well, tossing and turning, wondering if maybe I should have held back some. It was just so perfect with the prophet opening that door for me, and I figured there was no time like then, but the fear that I went off the deep end was there.

When morning came Roy decided to call me instead of texting. He said, "I just want you to know everything is okay. I'm fine with all of it. I needed some time to think. We're good babe; we're good." Those words were music to my ears.

We continued dating, which soon turned to courting, because we both knew we were getting married. My dad, who lives with me, took a real liking to Roy. My kids and my grandkids began to treat him as family. Each day, we grew more and more knit together. Each day, it became more and more difficult to say goodnight and part.

I was 53 at the time and so was Roy. He had his own apartment a few blocks from where I worked. It would have been very convenient to hang out there and then be five minutes from work in the morning. Never once did I stay at his apartment. As a matter of fact, I only went there two times for five minutes each time. Instead, he came to my house every night.

There was never a thought of me going there and staying there, not even once. We didn't have the mindset that we were in our 50s and could do what we wanted. Even if we would have done it for the simple convenience of it, it would have had a different appearance and the Scripture in *I Thessalonians 5:22* instructs us to "Abstain from all appearance of evil." Yes, I was 53 and I cared what my dad and my children would think. And you know what? I'm proud of it!

After a few months, Roy and I were talking and we came to the conclusion that if this was all ordained from the Master, then why shouldn't we just get married? Cool idea, we both thought. Me, being that ole' schoolgirl that I am, got frightened because now I realized we would have to tell my dad, so I suggested that Roy would go and talk to my brother, Pastor Peter (without me) and that he would also tell Dad (without me).

Roy laughed at me, but agreed to do it. In the meantime, Roy was asking me questions about a ring if I were to get one. I explained that I didn't really need a ring but if he was going to buy me one, I liked diamonds! He laughed.

CHAPTER EIGHT

ENGAGED

"I will praise Thee, O Lord, among the people: and I will sing praises unto Thee among the nations. For Thy mercy is great above the heavens: and Thy truth reacheth unto the clouds. Be Thou exalted, O God, above the heavens: and Thy glory above all the earth;"

Psalm 108: 3-5 (KJV)

"Lord, You have assigned me my portion and my cup; You have made my lot secure. The boundary lines have fallen for me in pleasant places: surely I have a delightful inheritance. I will praise the Lord, who counsels me; even at night my heart instructs me. I have set the Lord always before me."

Psalm 16: 5-8 (NIV)

A Match Made In Heaven

Engaged

Every time Roy came to pick me up to go out, he would have a rose behind his back. Other times, I would get a bouquet of flowers or plants and gifts sent to work. The very first gift I received from Roy was a little gold and ceramic bookmark that said, "You Are Special."

It was so nice. I felt as if I were a young girl, all smitten and lovesick. Whoever said love was only for the young? Love sure does not have an age limit. I never thought I could be so comfortable and as relaxed as I was with Roy. I was able to just be me, and that is so important in a relationship.

While I was being blessed and having such fun, I felt burdened for the young girls around me, the ones who desired a life partner and to start families. I felt badly because I was getting blessed at my age with a second chance at love and happiness. I had the privilege of knowing love, being cared for and raising a family. Now, God was blessing me again. And this time, it was even better than before! When God brings restoration, He always does abundantly above that which we could ask or think. *(See Ephesians 3:20)* It's just the way God operates.

We hadn't picked a date for marriage yet, but we were discussing it. I was waiting for Roy to talk with my brother and my dad. I was such a chicken little. What was my problem? I knew they both approved of Roy, but I couldn't help thinking that they would say it was way too soon to actually get married.

Then I reasoned with myself that I was acting ridiculous. If God put His stamp of approval on it, then there wasn't anything to fear. The two-year rule, one that many marriage advisers suggest, is a good one. You should definitely have the time to get to know someone with whom you are going to spend the rest of your life. However, there are exceptions to every rule, and I guess at our age God was gracious to make this exception.

One night, Roy came in from a Monday night Bible study that my brother, Pastor Peter, was teaching. I asked him if he'd like something to eat. He said, "Yes," so I proceeded to heat up his food in the toaster oven. While standing in front of the toaster oven and preparing the rest of his dish, he came from behind me.

Wrapping his arms around me, in front of me he held a little box. I was shocked not expecting to see that; there wasn't even a tiny inkling in my thoughts. I opened the pretty little box and found an engagement ring that was just my taste.

When Roy placed it on my finger, we realized it fit perfectly. Yes, (you guessed correctly again), it was a diamond ring with princess-cut diamonds--so beautiful!! I was pleasantly surprised. That was the nicest "real" surprise I ever experienced.

After I jumped around about my new ring, Roy informed me that he spoke to my brother after the

Bible study. He explained that he told him our plans about getting married *real soon*. My brother expressed that, although it was "kind of soon" he knew it "was right" and he gave us his blessings. He told Roy to just call the office to make sure they hold the date for him to do the wedding.

Years back, when I would go to the mall, I would gaze at the jewelry windows and admire engagement rings. While staring, I would always sense the Lord's sweet anointing, (His Presence). I remember being puzzled at the moving in of the presence of the Lord. I was seriously only gazing and nothing more. I was not thinking of ever receiving a ring nor was I fantasizing about getting engaged.

I gather, all those times at the mall window shopping, the Lord was showing me I was going to have a ring. What a caring God. The sweet presence of the Holy Spirit goes with us when we shop or even when we just window shop. He knows our every thought and He really does do "abundantly above all we could ask or think."

From that night, the ring was always on my finger. Folks from work and church noticed it. "What is that on your finger?" was the question of the day. I showed off the ring to all who asked. At this time, my dad, didn't know this new information. We hadn't even told him we were getting married and now we were officially engaged.

A Match Made In Heaven

Roy said, "Come on; go tell your dad." I reminded him that he said he would do it. So, he said, "Okay, we'll do it together."

"All right," I responded. So the next time Dad was in the room with us, Roy told him that we got engaged and I showed Dad the ring. My dad was thrilled and very excited. He just wasn't delighted when he found out he wasn't the first to be told. However, he readily forgave us with the thought of the excitement that he was going to walk me down the aisle again. I sighed with relief. Now that Dad knew that we were officially engaged to be married, all my fear dissipated. I began to just enjoy being engaged.

We got engaged in November and began planning a spring wedding. I was forever singing that ole' church song, "There's gonna be a wedding and the bride's getting ready for the groom..." I always sang that song at work when someone was getting married. Now, I was singing it for myself. Of course, the song was written about Christ marrying his bride, the Church, but years ago it was a favorite played at Christian weddings.

One day, my boss' daughter entered my office. I looked at her while I was singing the song. Then I said to her, under the inspiration of the Holy Spirit, "First me, and then you. Right after me, I'm going to be singing this song for you."

She was a sweet young girl in her early 20s, desiring a husband and family. She looked at me and giggled.

Engaged

She was married a year and a half after me, and now has two beautiful little boys. That is one prophetic song: "There's gonna be a wedding, and the bride's getting ready for the groom..."

A Match Made In Heaven

CHAPTER NINE

THE WEDDING

"May He give you the desire of your heart and make all your plans succeed. We will shout for joy when you are victorious and will lift up our banners in the name of our God. May the Lord grant all your requests. Now I know that the Lord saves His anointed; He answers him from His holy heaven with the saving power of His right hand. Some trust in chariots and some in horses, but we trust in the name of the Lord our God."

Psalm 20:4-7(NIV)

A Match Made In Heaven

The Wedding

*W*e set the wedding date for March 25, 2006. On the cruise the prophet had said, "Next year at this time," and just as he prophesied, so it was. What an exciting year. From the cruise to the wedding, there was one day of excitement after another.

Now, we were preparing for the big day, where we would take our vows before God and man. I wanted it to be a day that would truly glorify God. So, although we just had a quaint dinner party planned for the immediate family and close friends, we encouraged all those we were in contact with to attend the church to witness the exchanging of our vows.

I waited on the Lord's direction for what songs to play at the wedding. This was very serious to me; I wanted lives to be touched. God moved on me to play the inspiring hymn "Great is Thy Faithfulness" and also the song "Above All," which is a favorite of both Roy and mine.

After the inspiration came from the Lord, I informed those at church who would be taking care of that part of the ceremony. I was fortunate that my sister-in-law Teresa, Pastor Peter's wife, was a leader in the music ministry at church for years. Therefore, she had at her fingertips great versions to the songs I chose.

At first, I was just going to buy a nice plain dress, but my soon-to-be husband handed me money one day and said, "This is for your dress." While shopping with my two daughters and trying on simple dresses, they informed me that those weren't cutting it. They instructed me to "buy a wedding dress."

"Really?" I responded. I thought that would be silly to do. After shopping in many different shops, we decided to try, just one more place. We found the right dress in that last shop. The woman who worked there was very helpful. She informed us that a certain dress had just come in and she "knew it would be perfect for me."

It had not yet been put out for display, so she had to go in the back of the store to get it. It wasn't too plain and it wasn't too frilly. When I tried it on, my daughters informed me that it was "the one" and that I was "buying it." Knowing I had to obey my daughters, I asked the woman for the sales price, and to my surprise, it was exactly the amount that Roy had given me to buy a dress. It was a wedding dress, and it was waiting for me.

I didn't expect to get a shower and I refused to participate in a bridal registry. However, my daughter Janine registered for me. She picked all the things she knew I could use. And who knows a mom's taste better than a daughter? What a nice surprise bridal shower I was given! I got to meet more of Roy's family that day. It was wonderful! Everyone showered me with gifts and good wishes. The women at work also threw me a surprise bridal shower. I was blessed with much affection and love. I had two bridal showers, and hadn't expected one.

My sister Cherise, who is 19 years younger than me, showered me with gifts and attention along with my daughters. My sister was only a year old the first time I got married. I had always asked my parents for a baby sister, but three times they brought home baby brothers. After many years, my baby sister arrived. She was more like a daughter to me. She was too young to remember my first bridal shower. Now, at this present family bridal shower, she was right there assisting me in the opening of my gifts. Along with her, were her two daughters (who are more like granddaughters than nieces), my two daughters and my granddaughters. Very blessed seems inadequate for how I felt.

The wedding day arrived. The honeymoon was set, the dinner party was set, the church was set. Some of my friends came by the night before with my sister and daughters and we had a Chinese dinner and a lot of laughs. They helped me over pack for the honeymoon. Shelia was right there recounting the funny story of the way God brought me and Roy together. She said she was sure glad that I finally knew the man's last name. We had a real good time that night.

The church ceremony was set for 11 in the morning. I awoke and proceeded to get ready. I kept crying and crying. I had to keep re-applying mascara because I was weeping so. I realized the pain in the very gut of me was the fact that my mom was not able to join us. Oh how I missed her so. She would have been jumping for joy had she been with us. She took my divorce to heart. I think it hurt her more than it hurt me. No one, other than Jesus, gave me as much compassion as my mom.

When I would cry, she would comfort me and cry with me. I will never forget her loving hand upon my head telling me it was going to be all right. I didn't expect her missing presence would hit me as hard as it did and I was concerned how I would get my makeup on in time. I had to cry it out and thus, I did.

Then I called my sister and before I could talk, she said, "I know, I know" and started weeping, too. (I was 50 when my mom went home to be with the Lord; my sister was only beginning her 30s. While it hurts at any age to lose a mother, at younger ages it's even more difficult. I felt for her, because at least I had a half-century with my mom.) So, for a few minutes, while on the phone, we both cried and consoled each other as we missed Mom.

Later, my daughter Janine and niece Jill came by to help me get dressed and complete my makeup. They enabled me to pull it all together and get to the church.

I hadn't spoken to my brother Peter, (who would be marrying us), about the wedding ceremony. I trusted he would be led by the Lord,

The Wedding

as he always is, and knew he would do a great job. When I greeted him before the ceremony began, I asked him to announce something. I had forgotten to include in the invitations--the directions to the restaurant. So, I asked him if he could mention that I had placed them at the back of the church. "If I remember," he responded. "This is very difficult for me to do today."

I didn't understand his response, so I expressed his reply to my sister, Cherise. She understood immediately. "He's talking about Mommy," she said. "He's feeling what we are feeling."

Cherise was indeed correct. Peter preached an awesome message titled, "A Mother's Prayers." He shared that he knew my mom prayed for this day that we were experiencing, and expounded on how God hears the prayers of a mother. There were many wet eyes in the church that day. Many were touched by the message and the ceremony.

God was glorified in multiple ways. I was reminded of how my mom wanted nothing but happiness for me. She would always tell me how she was in her "prayer closet" talking to God about changes in my life. It was as if my mom's presence was with us on my wedding day.

As my brother was preaching, I vividly remembered all her words of comfort and prayers for me. Roy's mother was also a praying woman. She shared that she had been praying for years for his happiness and for him to meet someone special. As she sat on the front row of the church, she said she was blessed to hear that both mothers took part in bringing together our union.

We are co-laborers with God *(I Corinthians 3:9)*, and prayer in the powerful name of Jesus changes things. We had a wonderful wedding where God's name was lifted up. All the folks we invited to witness our vows were there. To our pleasant surprise, others showed up, whom we didn't invite, but just wanted to share in our joy.

The church was filled with people from both mine and Roy's lives. When the preacher proclaimed, "And now for the first time on this side of heaven, Mr. and Mrs. Roy Wolmart!" the crowd roared. We could feel the joy in the air. What a mighty God we serve!

CHAPTER TEN

THAT STILL SMALL VOICE

"He maketh me to lie down in green pastures: He leadeth me beside the still waters. He restoreth my soul: He leadeth me in the paths of righteousness for His name's sake." "Surely goodness and mercy shall follow me all the days of my life..."

Psalm 23:2,3,6 (KJV)

A Match Made In Heaven

That Still Small Voice

As I mentioned at the beginning of this short book, I was commissioned by God to share my story. Thus, I obeyed God's *gentle inner prompting, His "still small Voice"* and wrote my story. The fact that God inspired me to write a book leads me to believe there are others, who for one reason or another, needed to hear my testimony. For some, it may have been to simply read about *the goodness of God,* and if so, praise Him. Perhaps others may have needed some encouragement on their single journey.

I hope you enjoyed taking this short journey with me. More importantly, I hope that you discovered the importance of having a *relationship* with God because He is not unapproachable or unreachable. Rather, he is a very present God who wants to be involved in every aspect of our lives. If we are listening for Him, we will learn to discern His promptings and He will enable us by His grace to follow Him.

Had it not been for God's grace, words of wisdom and guidance for my life, I would have failed greatly. I have found the Lord's grace very rich. His "still small Voice" within has prompted me to take opportunities that helped pave my way through life. I am burdened that so many do not know God's "still small Voice." So many seek outside counsel, when the answer is within.

A Match Made In Heaven

Hebrews 8:11 (KJV) says *"... for all shall know Me, from the least to the greatest."* *I John 2:27 (KJV)* also says *"...the anointing which you have received of Him abides in you, and you need not that any man teach you: but as the same anointing teaches you of all things... "*

What if you don't know what to do and you don't know what God is saying? Wait on God because He is always on time. What about the times when you have to make a decision and you just aren't sure the way to go? Make a decision. If you prayed and asked Jesus for direction believe me, He will intervene if the decision is wrong. I have been at closing tables when purchasing and selling homes, and other times close to closing tables when everything fell apart. [That may be another book someday!] There were times I prayed and although the answer didn't come when I wanted it to, it did arrive right in the nick of time.

"My times are in Thy hand..." it says in *Psalm 31:15,* and if we believe that, we will see God come in like a flood for us at the perfect, precise moment. There have been countless times, God came and transformed my situation. Over the past 35 plus years, I have learned through every circumstance and situation, even when it looks contrary, to rejoice. As I've learned more about God and grown closer to Him, it has become easier to trust Him for everything. Now, I celebrate when that "gentle whisper" intervenes and redirects and makes the way straight.

98

That Still Small Voice

I know that His ways are higher than my ways and that His way is the better way! When I was first *saved,* a preacher lady once taught me to "Get in God's way." She assured me that if you want Him to lead you, you just get in His way and be certain that He will correct you and change the path if it's not the right road.

Finally, I want to make it very clear that in no way am I trying to uncover or share anything negative about my ex-husband. I truly believe it takes two people to make a marriage and two people to break a marriage. I take responsibility for the part I played in the breakup of my first marriage. Unless there are extreme circumstances where abuse is happening, it is never God's will for a marriage to split.

Jesus teaches us in *Matthew 19:5-8,* that from the beginning it was not so. He explained that when a man and a woman are joined in marriage, they become one flesh and nothing should separate that union. Jesus goes on to explain that Moses allowed divorce only because of the hardness, the stubbornness and perversity of people's hearts (as the *Amplified Bible* reads).

I believe the powers of darkness came against my first marriage as they do many marriages. There are demons who are assigned by Satan to destroy the institution of marriage that God created. Marriage symbolizes Christ and His bride, the Church--something the devil hates. Breaking down a marriage means breaking down a family and that gives the devils much pleasure.

Demonic powers are very subtle. My ex-husband and I were too blind to realize what was taking place. The enemy sometimes wins a battle, but in the end we win the war. As a matter of fact, it is written that we have already won! That finished work at Calvary, the death and resurrection of our Savior, secured our victory, of which no marriage breakup can interfere. I also believe the will and purpose of God will be done in our lives.

We simply cannot mess up so much that God cannot restore and rebuild and do what He purposed in our lives. That's the kind of God we serve. He paid the price with His own blood for our every mess-up and every failure. He is truly the God of a second and third and fourth, and so on, chance.

The second point I would like to make is this: I beseech those of you who are entertaining the idea of separating to reconsider. I am deeply burdened that so many marriages are failing. The statistics in churches of failed marriages are startling. A recent survey by the National Opinion Research Center at the University of Chicago found that Christians in America have a divorce rate of 42 percent. Among the religiously unaffiliated, that rate is 50 percent, the survey said.

When we begin thinking that the grass will be greener with someone else, or we no longer feel as if we are in love with our spouses, know that sometimes those thoughts are demonic suggestions. Instead, pray and ask Jesus for the grace, wisdom and the agape (unconditional) love you need to stay and keep your covenant. God is more than willing to give you His abundant supply of these things. The Bible tells us in *James 1*:5, that if any of us lacks wisdom he should ask of the Lord who gives liberally to all men who ask in faith.

If you don't have faith to believe for wisdom, read what Jesus said about faith in *Luke 17:5 and 6.* Jesus' apostles asked Him how they could increase their faith. His answer was simple: "If you have faith even as a grain of mustard seed, you could say to this mulberry tree, be pulled up by the roots, and be planted in the sea, and it would obey you." (*Amplified Version*)

We used to sing a song years ago about faith that said, "You don't need a whole lot, just use what you got..." Every marriage needs prayer. Every marriage needs work. The Apostle Paul taught us in *I Corinthians 7:28* that in marriage we would "have physical and earthly troubles..." (*Amplified Version*) Every relationship needs consistent work. It's not easy for two people to flow in the stresses of everyday life. However, "the things which are impossible with men are possible with God." (*KJV Luke 18:27*)

I sometimes wish that in the early days of my first marriage, I knew what I know now. However, that isn't possible. For that is who I was then, and this is who I am now and tomorrow I hope to have more wisdom and more insight. For we are ever changing and growing, increasing in wisdom, stature and in the knowledge of God. The more we see Him the more we can become like Him. We go from glory to glory and from faith to faith. It's a growing process.

"For precept must be upon precept; line upon line; here a little, and there a little:" (*Isaiah 28: 10 KJV*) I am so thankful there is "no condemnation to them who are in Christ Jesus." (*Romans 8:1*) I am so grateful that we could learn from our mistakes and go on to be all God has created us and called us to be. We can also learn from the mistakes of others and be spared from the same error.

I hope this little message speaks to some of you on the fence about divorce. Don't do it! God can fix it! He is a restorer; a repairer and a builder up of old waste places. God wants to be glorified in your marriage.

Third, for those of you who desire to be married, you desire a good thing. Have your antennas up and make sure you choose someone with whom you are equally yoked. Make sure you choose someone who will not interfere with your passion for Christ and His kingdom. Don't rush into anything. Make sure you sense the inward peace of the Holy Spirit within you bearing witness to your choice. Will that mean you will live in Utopia? Certainly not. There is no such thing. You will, however, have a good foundation to stand on when "life happens" and trials come. And, they *WILL* come. You will be better equipped to stand against the wiles of the enemy when the enemy forms weapons against you. You will have a better sensing to get up and say, "NO you don't. Get under my feet in Jesus' name!"

Young ladies, I have a heart for you and I pray many of you will meet *Mr. Right* and raise families. I am so proud of many of you, whom I personally know, that you do not settle and are waiting for the *right* person. I pray in Jesus' name that this will be your year. I hope that reading this book has sparked faith in many of you and that you too will have a testimony that will bring God glory.

For others in a similar situation, facing a divorce and the end of a marriage that I shared at the beginning of this book, I pray a special grace to learn to be *alone* and depend on the God who created the heavens and the earth. Do not seek to fill your pain with anything other than His love and peace.

He is truly a merciful high priest who has been touched with your infirmities and knows and feels your pain. He is able to sympathize with your weaknesses. In order for Him to identify with us, He too was tempted in every way, just as you may be. *(See Hebrews 4: 15-16)* All you need to do is what the Scripture here tells us to do, and that is to approach the throne of grace with confidence, knowing that you will receive mercy and find grace to help in your time of need, for He cares for you.

You can come boldly to the throne as it says because you are going in that powerful name of Jesus and there isn't anything God the Father won't do for Jesus. He gave us that name to pray in and covered us with His blood. Every sin, every weakness and every shortcoming has been blotted out because of that act at Calvary when Jesus so willingly went to the cross. When God the Father sees you, He sees Jesus, so be bold and believe largely and watch God do abundantly above all that you could ask or think. He did it for me and He'll do it for you.

"Only believe," were two of Jesus' favorite words. In *Hebrews 11:6 (KJV),* we read: "...for he that cometh to God must believe that He is, and that He is a rewarder of them that diligently seek Him." Believe that when you call on Him, He will answer. Believe He will come to your aid. Release that mustard seed of faith and reach out to your Creator who loves you so much He gave His life for you. Thus you will receive that "reward," which is His voice and direction to your life. So come to Him. He is waiting for you with open arms.

Indeed, there is a way that seems right unto a man but the end of it oftentimes, is destruction. The only way to prevent making the wrong choices is to follow His way. God is faithful to show us that way in which we are to go. In *John 10:27 (KJV)* Jesus says: "My sheep hear My voice, and I know them, and they follow Me." If you *listen* for Him, if you *talk* to Him, if you *express* your heart to Him and *ask* for His *guidance* and *direction,* you *will know* the way. "And thine ears shall hear a word behind thee, saying, this is the way, walk ye in it..." *Isaiah 30:21 (KJV)*

I hope my message and testimony has blessed you. I hope you are now saying with me, "To God Be the Glory!" My sincere prayer is that God would continue to richly bless you.

If you don't know Jesus as your Lord and Savior, do ask Him to come into your heart. Acknowledge that you believe He paid for your sins and sicknesses at Calvary. He became the once and for all sacrifice, so you could have access to the throne of God, have eternal life and life more abundantly here on earth also. Acknowledge that you believe God raised Jesus from the dead and that He now sits at the right hand of the Father. Acknowledge that you receive the unmerited favor and pardon for every sin you ever committed and are to commit, and begin a life experiencing the love of God as you never thought possible. Believe me, you will never be the same!

A Match Made In Heaven

EPILOGUE

A MESSAGE FROM ROY WOLMART

Years of experiencing life's disappointments had caused me to weaken and make some poor choices. Trying to ease the pain led me to a season of doing drugs. It wasn't long after, I found myself destitute and homeless.

But I knew the Lord. I had roots in God having come from generations of Holy Ghost believers; I knew the loving hand of the Father God was upon me. I had witnessed His hand get me out of many tough situations. I had several encounters where I knew angels were intervening on my behalf. I would often sense the prayers of my parents and family members.

Finally, at my lowest point, I heard God's "Voice," which my wife speaks about in this book. That voice instructed me to leave California and go home to my family in New York. One phone call to Mom and Dad, and there was a ticket waiting for me at the airport. I arrived in Long Island, N.Y., (where my wife also lived) at age 47. My whole family was there waiting for me with open arms. That was 1999, the same year my wife's devastating divorce began.

After a season of detox, rehabilitation and regaining my health, I started to attend church, (the same church my wife was attending). I rededicated my life to the Lord. I sat in the back of the church with a family that taught me how to worship. I began to experience God in a new way, just as the Scripture says, "He's new and fresh every morning."

In time, I was asked to join the ushers' ministry and help out in the house of the Lord. For years, I ushered in the back section of the church. I had never seen my wife, nor had she noticed me. We attended and probably passed each another, but never noticed each other. It wasn't time. God was working on us, healing us and preparing us for each other—making us whole.

A Match Made In Heaven

At some point, I began to pray for God to bring me a wife. I wanted companionship, but I wanted it to be the *right* person. After meeting my wife, we discovered that we were praying for a partner at the exact time!

Then I was assigned to usher in a new section at the front of the church, where my wife always sat. The first day in that section, Theresa wasn't there. (She was on the church cruise she mentions early in the book.) When she returned the next week and walked down the aisle, I led her to her seat. I didn't know that day that she was *the one*. Soon after, the chemistry between us was evident. That chemistry began to grow and became very intense. You know what happened after that. You just read the story!

We were praying at the same time for a mate. Our moms were praying for us to meet someone. It was a win-win. My mom once shared with me that she had a dream that I married a woman with dark hair. My wife has dark hair!

I give all the glory to God for His goodness and favor. I have a saying that I have brought into my life with Theresa and I often say to her: "Do you know whose we are?" What I mean is simply this: When you know you belong to the Father and that you are covered in the blood of His Son Jesus, nothing is impossible. Rather, anything IS possible. God Bless.

A Match Made In Heaven

Theresa would like to know your thoughts.
Email her at *theresawolmart@aol.com* or
find her on *facebook* as *Theresa Wolmart* or
A Match Made in Heaven

A Match Made In Heaven

A Match Made In Heaven

A Match Made In Heaven

www.ingramcontent.com/pod-product-compliance
Lightning Source LLC
Chambersburg PA
CBHW051839040426
42447CB00006B/613